Titles in this series
Big J
Clever Cleo
Don't Say No To Flo
Gunpowder Guy
Hal the Hero
The Little Queen
Will's Dream
William's Words

Text copyright © Stewart Ross 2002
Illustrations copyright © Sue Shields 2002

Series concept: Stewart Ross
Series editor: Alex Woolf
Editor: Liz Gogerly
Book design: Design Systems

The Publisher would like to thank Mary Evans for kind permission to use the photograph on page 30 of Florence Nightingale after her return from the Crimea.

Published in Great Britain by Hodder Wayland,
an imprint of Hodder Children's Books

British Library Cataloguing in Publication Data
Ross, Stewart
    Don't Say No To Flo : the story of Florence Nightingale. - (Stories from history)
    1. Nightingale, Florence, 1820–1910 2. Nurses – Great Britain – Biography – Juvenile literature 3. Nursing – Great Britain – History – 19th century – Juvenile literature 4. Crimean War, 1853–1856 – Juvenile literature
    I. Title II.Shields, Susan
    610. 7'3' 092

ISBN 0 7502 2502 5

Printed and bound in Hong Kong by Sheck Wah Tong Printing Press Ltd

Hodder Children's Books
A division of Hodder Headline Limited
338 Euston Road, London NW1 3BH

Don't Say No To Flo!

Stewart Ross
Illustrated by Sue Shields

HODDER
Wayland

an imprint of Hodder Children's Books

Flo looked in her paper.

There was a war!

Soldiers were very sick.

No one cared for them.

Flo wanted to help.

She got money …

and she got nurses.

Flo and her nurses went to the war.

They came to the army hospital.

Flo spoke to the boss.

The boss did not want Flo's help.

Flo and her nurses had to wait.

More soldiers came.

The army hospital was full.

The boss asked Flo for help.

Flo and her nurses went to work.

They cleaned up the hospital.

Flo was now the boss!

She got lots of help from England.

The soldiers had better food …

and Flo cared for them.

She was the soldiers' friend.

Flo went to see the soldiers in the war.

The men were so pleased ...

to see the soldiers' friend.

Do you know?

This story is TRUE!
Flo was FLORENCE NIGHTINGALE.
FLORENCE NIGHTINGALE was born in 1820.
She died in 1910.
This is what she looked like:

Notes for adults

Don't Say No To Flo! and the National Curriculum

Don't Say No To Flo! may be enjoyed in its own right or, in school, as part of a programme of reading and study linked to the National Curriculum. To this end, the language, content and presentation have been devised to meet the requirements of the *National Literacy Strategy* and *Key Stage 1 English and History*. Whether read by an individual pupil or by the teacher out loud, *Don't Say No To Flo!* makes a stimulating addition to material available for the Literacy Hour. It skilfully combines development of the 'knowledge, skills and understanding' and 'breadth of study' required by the *English National Curriculum* (pp. 18–19) with 'chronological understanding', 'knowledge and understanding of events, people and changes in the past' and learning about 'the lives of significant men, women and children drawn from the history of Britain and the wider world' and 'past events from the history of Britain and the wider world' suggested in the *History National Curriculum* (p.16).

Suggested follow-up activities

1. Checking the child knows and can use words they might not have come across before. In particular:

soldier	hooray	shirt	smell	groan
army	wait	horrible	cook	moan
pooh	owl	sick	grub	
everyone	goodbye	nurse	dirt	
hospital	care	lamp	England	
trouble	hundred	cheers	enough	

2. Talking about pictures of tangible objects that survive from the time of Florence Nightingale, e.g. buildings (houses, railway stations, etc.), furniture, works of art and everyday objects such as jewellery. Discussing how we know about Victorian times, i.e. sources.

3. Explaining the exact dates of Florence's life and the meaning of 'century'.

4. Going further into aspects of Florence's work. e.g. The Crimean War, women and work, women and society, medical services, education, etc.

5. Comparing life in Florence's time with our own, e.g. clothing, health and disease, travel, housing, religion, etc.